RESCUING REESE

Cassidy Mae

Out in the country, in a tiny little cage, sat a poor little dog who had never known what it was like to be loved.

A one-year-old pit bull named Reese was all alone, cold, hungry, and sad. He never got to run and play like other dogs. The people who owned Reese didn't love him and they weren't very nice to him.

One day they took Reese for a drive. He didn't know where they were going. They dropped him off at a strange place filled with many cages and other dogs, and they left him! They didn't want Reese anymore. He was so afraid.

Where did my people go? ❓

❓ **Why did they leave me here?**

Reese once again was put into a tiny little cage all alone.

People came by and looked at Reese, and he was so afraid that he barked and barked until they went away. He watched as the people played with the other dogs. They seemed so happy. The people took those dogs and they never came back.

Would Reese ever be able to leave?

After a few weeks, Reese lost all hope.

He thought he would be stuck there forever. But one day someone came to visit. Reese barked and he jumped, but the visitor didn't go away.

He stopped barking and looked at this stranger, who smiled at him and said,

"Hi, Reese. I'm Deedee.   Will you let me be your friend?"

Deedee took Reese for a walk down a quiet dirt road. He stayed nicely by her side, but when she reached out to him, he turned away in fear.

"It's okay, Reese. 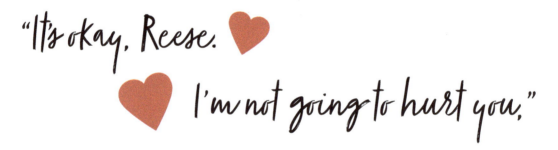 I'm not going to hurt you," Deedee said, and softly petted his back.

They passed by a house where a man was outside doing yard work. When Reese saw him, he became so scared. He started barking and pulling, trying with all his might to get away. Deedee tried to calm him down, but poor Reese didn't trust anyone. He never wanted to get hurt again.

Deedee sat with Reese in his kennel and gently petted his back. She said,

"You're a good boy. You're going to be okay."

Reese looked at her with his big eyes and jumped into her lap, covering her face in big, slobbery kisses. She fell backwards, laughing and crying with joy.

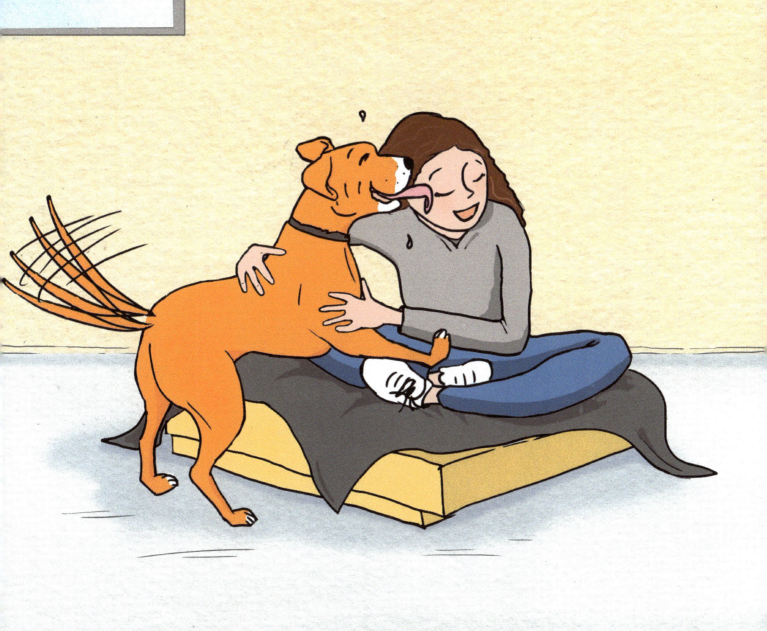

Deedee visited Reese often, taking him for walks and sitting with him in his kennel. Even though he was an hour away from her, she came as often as she could and stayed as long as possible. Every time she left, it was harder to say goodbye and Reese hated watching her leave.

The next week Deedee came back, but this time she brought her dad. She told him not to expect to be able to get very close to Reese. At first when Reese saw Deedee's dad, he was so scared, jumping and barking. He kept his distance, and it was a long time before Reese was calm.

Deedee's dad sat down, and Reese watched him carefully. He moved closer, sniffing her dad's shoes. When Reese became relaxed, Deedee's dad reached out his hand. He gave Reese a pat on the back, and Reese jumped into his arms, licking his face. Reese was such a loving and sweet boy, he was just too scared to show it.

This time when *Deedee* said goodbye at the kennel, it was for the last time. *Reese* watched her go, whining as she left. He spent the next few weeks sad and alone. He had no visitors, and nobody wanted to take him. Maybe this was his home now, maybe he would never get to leave.

But one day, as Reese sat alone in the kennel, he heard someone come in. He waited to see who it was, hoping it might be somebody that would want to play with him. When he finally saw who it was, Reese jumped in the air with excitement.

It was Deedee. She came back!

"Hi, Reese. I'm going to take you home."

Reese jumped into her arms, covering her face in big, slobbery kisses. He couldn't believe she was back, and she was taking him home! This was the best day of his life. He was never going to be hurt by anyone ever again. Reese was safe and would finally be able to run and play like other dogs.

Reese got in the car with his new mom who would love him forever. With Reese's head out the window and his ears flapping in the wind, they headed to their new home. This was just the beginning of a beautiful friendship and so many wonderful adventures for Reese and Deedee.

Cassidy Mae is an artist, photographer, musician, and dog lover.

She rescued the real-life Reese after volunteering at an animal shelter and falling in love with bully breeds. These days, she lives in Halifax, Nova Scotia, with her dog, Rey.

Read Cassidy's experiences on her blog, **reesesnpieces.com**.

FriesenPress

One Printers Way
Altona, MB R0G 0B0
Canada

www.friesenpress.com

Copyright © 2022 by Cassidy Mae
First Edition — 2022

All rights reserved.

Illustrations by Val Lawton

No part of this publication may be reproduced in any form, or by any means, electronic or mechanical, including photocopying, recording, or any information browsing, storage, or retrieval system, without permission in writing from FriesenPress.

ISBN
978-1-03-914642-6 (Hardcover)
978-1-03-914641-9 (Paperback)
978-1-03-914643-3 (eBook)

1. JUVENILE NONFICTION, ANIMALS, DOGS

Distributed to the trade by The Ingram Book Company